W9-AKE-966

Baby Animals

Einstein Sisters

KidsWorld

A baby black bear is **called a cub**. A **group of bears** is called a **sloth**.

Sometimes **black bears** stand up on two legs to sniff the air. They have a good **sense of smell**. Black bears are big but they can **run very fast**.

Black bears have **short claws**. They are very good at **climbing trees**.

A baby tiger is called a **cub**. **Tiger cubs** stay with their **mother** until they are **two years old.**

The tiger is the **biggest member** of the cat family. A tiger can weigh as much as **four** people.

Tigers are good **swimmers.** They like to soak in streams or pools of water to cool off. Tigers usually **hunt alone** at night.

Tiger

An owl can't move its eyes, so it has to **turn** its head. An owl can turn its head almost all the way around to the back.

A baby owl is **called an owlet.**
Owls are found everywhere except Antarctica.
A group of owls is called a parliament.

Great Horned Owl

Owls are **most active at night.** They have **big eyes** to help them **see in the dark.**

Great horned owls **fly very quietly** and swoop down on their prey. They **eat** bugs, mice, snakes and small birds.

Foxes **dig dens** in the ground. They live in the same den for **many years.**

Red Fox

A baby fox is called a pup, a cub or a kit.
Foxes can climb trees. Sometimes they like to sit on low branches.
Foxes hunt at night. They have very good night vision.
Foxes eat small rodents like mice and rabbits. They catch them with a high pounce.

Elephant

A baby elephant is **called a calf.** A group of elephants is called **a herd.**

Elephants are the biggest land animals **in the world.** The elephant is the **only** animal that can't jump. Elephants are good **swimmers.**

Elephants only have **four teeth.** Each tooth is about the **size of a brick.**

Elephants **flap their ears** to keep themselves **cool.**

Kangaroo

Kangaroos can't walk backwards. **Kangaroos** can swim.

A baby kangaroo is called a joey. A joey is about the size of a **grape** when it is born. It lives in its mom's pouch until it is about 10 months old.

Kangaroos have **big, strong tails.** The tail helps them balance and turn **when** they hop.

Swan

A baby swan
is called a **cygnet**.
A **group** of swans is
called a **bevy**.

Swans eat
mostly plants.
Sometimes they eat
**bugs and
fish.**

A swan can
weigh 13 kilograms,
the same as a **small
human child!**
A pair of swans
stays together all
their lives.

A baby orangutan is **called an infant.** The infant stays with its mother for **11 or 12 years.**

Orangutans live in trees. They live in Borneo and Sumatra **in Asia.**

Orangutans
are not monkeys.
They are apes.
Orangutans eat mostly fruit.
They also eat nuts, bugs and eggs.
Orangutans can live to be
35 years old.

Orangutan

If a skunk is **angry or afraid**, it will turn around and lift its tail. Then it shoots a stinky spray at its attacker. Skunk spray smells really bad but it **doesn't hurt.**

A baby skunk is **called a kit.** A skunk is about the same size as a **cat.**

Skunks are **mostly active at night. They eat** bugs, worms, eggs, plants, berries and **even bees!**

Skunk

Ostrich

A baby ostrich is **called a chick.**
Ostriches can't fly but they can **run very fast.**
An ostrich can **live for 50 years.**
A group of ostriches is called a flock.

One ostrich egg **weighs** as much as **24 chicken** eggs.

Ostriches are the **biggest** and **heaviest** birds. An **ostrich can weigh** 180 kilograms—as much as **two people!**

A baby lynx **is called a kitten or cub.** Kittens stay with their mother for two years.

Big paws help the lynx walk on snow. A lynx can't run very fast so it **sneaks up on its prey.** Lynxes eat rabbits and other small animals. Lynxes **hunt at night** and can see well in the dark.

A lynx looks like a big house cat, but it has a very short tail. Lynxes live in the forest.

Lynx

Mustang

A baby mustang is called a foal. When it is two years old, a male mustang is called a colt and a female is called a filly.

Mustangs are descended from tame horses brought by Europeans more than 400 years ago.

Mustangs are small, wild horses. They have very strong legs and hard hooves.

Mustangs live in groups called herds. They eat mostly grass.

Rabbit

Baby rabbits are called **bunnies or kits.** They are born with **closed eyes** and **no fur.**

Rabbits can run **very fast.** They often run in a z^{i}g^{z}ag to escape animals that want to eat them. Rabbits have **strong legs** and can **jump very high.** A group of rabbits is **called a colony.**

Rabbits can see in front, to the sides and behind. When a rabbit **thumps its back leg,** it means there is **danger.**

A baby giraffe is **called a calf.** Giraffes are the tallest land mammals. They can be **5.5 metres tall.** That is almost as **tall as a house!**

A giraffe's **foot** is about the size of a **dinner plate.**

Giraffes don't need to drink every day. Most of their water comes from the **plants they eat.**

A giraffe's tongue is black and very **long.** It uses its tongue to pick leaves and branches. A giraffe can **pick its own nose** with its tongue!

Giraffe

A baby
porcupine is called
a porcupette.

Porcupines
have long, stiff hairs
called quills to protect them.
They have about 30,000
quills!

Porcupines like to climb trees. They eat leaves, twigs and bark. They love salt. Porcupines can't see very well, but they have a good sense of smell.

Porcupines are active mostly at night.

A group of porcupines is called a prickle.

Porcupine

A baby **zebra** is called a **foal**. Zebras live in **Africa**.

Each zebra has a different pattern of **black and white stripes**. The stripes are a kind of **camouflage**. When many zebras are together, **their stripes** make it hard for a predator to pick out one zebra to chase.

Zebras are in the same family as **horses and donkeys**. Zebras stand up while **sleeping**.

Zebra

Robins eat mostly **worms** in the summer and **berries** in the winter.

A baby bird that has just hatched is **called a hatchling. When** it is a bit older, it is called a nestling or fledgling.

When a robin stands still and **turns its head,** it is looking for worms moving under the grass.

Robin

Koala

A baby koala is called a joey. The joey lives in its mom's pouch for six months after it is born.

Koalas are not bears. They are marsupials, like kangaroos.

Koalas live **in Australia.** A group of koalas **is called** a colony.

Koalas live **in eucalyptus trees.** They only eat **eucalyptus leaves.**

Emperor Penguin

The mother penguin lays only one egg. The father takes care of the egg. He keeps it warm between his feet.
There are 17 kinds of penguins. The emperor penguin is the biggest.

Penguins have more feathers than any other bird. Penguins can't fly but they are very good swimmers.

A baby penguin is called a chick.

Grey Wolf

A group of wolves is called a pack. All members of the pack take care of the pups. Pups have blue eyes when they are born. Their eyes change colour after a few months. Most wolves have yellow eyes.

A baby wolf is called a pup.

Wolves belong to the dog family. A wolf can run as fast as a car!

A lion's **roar** is very loud. You can hear it **8 kilometres** away!

Lions rest about 20 hours each day. **They hunt at night.** The **lionesses** do most of the hunting. Only male lions have manes. The oldest lions have the **darkest manes.**

A baby lion is **called a cub.** The lion is the **second largest cat** in the the world. Lions **live in Africa.**

Lion

Harp seals can stay underwater for **15 minutes.** They eat fish, crabs, lobsters and shrimp. A group of seals is **called a pod or herd.**

Baby seals are **called pups.** The pups have **soft, white fur.**

Harp seals live in **the Arctic.** A thick layer of fat under their fur **keeps them warm.**

Harp Seal

Bald Eagle

Bald eagles are big. A bald eagle's wings **stretch** out 2 metres. The female eagle is **bigger than** the male. A pair of eagles stays together all their lives.

A baby eagle is called an eaglet. Eagles, hawks, falcons and owls are called "birds of prey."

A bald eagle isn't really **bald**, its head is just **white**. Bald eagles like to eat fish, other birds, ducks, muskrats and sometimes turtles.

Ducks have waterproof feathers. Ducks' feet can't feel cold, so ducks are comfortable walking on ice and swimming in cold water.

Ducks eat plants, fish and bugs. Sometimes they tip upside down and eat plants underwater. Ducks swim well because of their webbed feet.

A baby duck is called a duckling. Ducklings can run and swim a day after they hatch.

Mallard Duck

Cheetah

The cheetah is the **fastest** land animal in the world. It can run more than **110 kilometres per hour.** That's as fast as a car on **a highway!**

A baby cheetah is called **a cub.**

Cheetahs can't roar like lions, but they can **purr, hiss and growl.** Cheetahs **don't have** sharp claws, so **they can't climb trees.** **Unlike most cats,** cheetahs can't see very well at night. They hunt during the day.

Moose

Moose are good swimmers. They eat plants. Sometimes they dive underwater to eat plants at the bottom of a lake.

The moose is the biggest member of the deer family. Only male moose have antlers.

A baby moose is called a calf.

Deer

Fawns have a **reddish-brown coat** with about **300 white spots.**
Fawns don't have any smell, so predators can't find them. If a fawn is in danger, it stays perfectly still.

Deer can
run **very fast.**
They can also jump up to
3 metres high.

A baby
deer is **called
a fawn.**

Deer
are very good
swimmers.

Polar
Bear

Polar bears are the biggest predators on land. They are also the largest bears. Polar bears only live in the Arctic. They mostly eat seals. Polar bears are very good swimmers.

A baby polar bear is called a cub.

A polar bear's fur is not white. The hairs are clear and hollow like tiny straws.

Polar bears have black skin. The skin absorbs heat and helps keep the bear warm.

Monkey

Monkeys have thumbs like people do. Most animals don't have thumbs.

There are more than 260 different kinds of monkeys. Some monkeys **live on the ground** and others **live in trees.** Most monkeys have long, powerful tails. They **use their tails** to hang from branches or to hold on to things.

Monkeys yawn when they are angry.

A baby monkey is **called an infant,** just like a human baby. A group of monkeys is **called a troop.**

Canada Goose

Canada geese
are found all over
Canada and the US. They
eat grass and grain.
They really like
blueberries.

Some Canada geese
fly south when it gets cold.
Flocks of geese fly in a "V" shape.
Canada geese can fly more
than 2000 kilometres
in one day.

A baby
goose is called
a gosling.
Goslings can swim
as soon as they
hatch.

Cougars have very powerful legs. They can jump 5.5 metres high. That's as **high as a house!** Cougars stalk their prey and pounce on it when they are close. They eat rabbits, squirrels, deer and birds.

Cougar cubs have spots and stripes that fade as they get older.

A baby cougar is **called a cub.** A cougar is also called **a mountain lion or puma.**

Cougar

The Publisher: KidsWorld Books

Library and Archives Canada Cataloguing in Publication

Baby animals / Einstein Sisters.

ISBN 978-0-9938401-6-6 (pbk.)

1. Animals—Infancy—Juvenile literature. I. Einstein Sisters, author

QL763.B32 2014   j591.3'92   C2014-903889-5

Cover Images: Front cover: rabbit, MikeLane45 / Thinkstock. *Back cover:* kangaroo, John Camemolla / Thinkstock; orangutan, Enjoylife2 / Thinkstock; fawn, HIRO-amanaimagesRF / Thinkstock.
Background Graphics: abstract swirl, hakkiarslan / Thinkstock, 4, 9, 18, 27, 31, 39, 48; abstract background, Maryna Borsevych / Thinkstock, 3, 14, 28, 41, 56, 62; pixels, Misko Kordic / Thinkstock, 6, 12, 17, 20, 22, 32, 36, 42, 44, 47, 54, 59.
Photo Credits: Michael Gäbler / Wikipedia, 52. From Thinkstock: Anolis01, 48–49; bach005, 16; Cheryl Davis, 34, 34–35; Comstock Images, 44, 47; csterken, 6; Elizabeth Hoffman, 20; Enjoylife2, 17; Evgenia, 76, 58; fouroaks, 32; Fuse, 38; hilton kotze, 51; HIRO-amanaimagesRF, 55; Holly Kuchera, 41; hurricanehank, 43; IPGGutenbergUKLtd, 62; JanJJ, 15; Jason Prince, 29; Jeff McGraw, 8; JHWilliams, 53; Jim Larson, 61; John Carnemolla, 12; John Pitcher, 31, 40, 56–57; Jupiterimages, 23; Kyslynskyy, 9; Lynn Bystrom, 3, 18–19; Marilyn Dunstan, 39; MarkMalkinsonPhotography, 4–5; Mike Watson Images, 7; MikeLane45, 22, 27, 59; NightOwlZA, 51; outcast85, 37; Palenque, 33; poetrygirl128, 61; predrag1, 46; pum_eva, 14, 42a; Purestock, 45, 63; Renate Smitham, 13; rogertrentham, 54; shane partridge, 36; skynavin, 4; TanzanianImages, 10–11; Tom Brakefield, 2, 30; webguzs, 42b; westernphotographs, 24–25; wolfavni, 21; Zoonar_S Heap, 26–27.

We acknowledge the financial support of the Government of Canada through the Canada Book Fund (CBF) for our publishing activities.

 Canadian   Patrimoine
Heritage   canadien

PC: 27